STARS OF SPORTS

ADAM THIELEN

FOOTBALL'S UNDERDOG STAR

by Matt Chandler

CAPSTONE PRESS
a capstone imprint

Stars of Sports is published by Capstone Press, an imprint of Capstone
1710 Roe Crest Drive, North Mankato, Minnesota 56003
www.capstonepub.com

**Library of Congress Cataloging-in-Publication Data is available on the Library of
Congress website.**
ISBN: 978-1-4966-8381-6 (hardcover)
ISBN: 978-1-4966-8432-5 (eBook PDF)

Summary: Adam Thielen always knew he wanted to play in the NFL. From growing up
watching Randy Moss and the Vikings to playing at a small Division II college, his path
to the NFL hasn't always been a straight line. After initially making the Vikings roster
in 2013, he was cut to the practice squad. Now, he's Minnesota's top wide receiver.
Learn more about Thielen's path to football fame.

Editorial Credits
Editor: Gena Chester; Designer: Sarah Bennett; Media Researcher: Eric Gohl;
Production Specialist: Laura Manthe

Image Credits
Associated Press: Charlie Neibergall, 17, Jim Mone, 19; Dreamstime: Cindy203, 8–9,
Jerry Coli, 6; Getty Images: Stringer/Hannah Foslien, 15, Tom Szczerbowski, 21;
Minnesota State University Athletics: 11, 13; Newscom: Icon Sportswire/Ric Tapia,
cover, Icon Sportswire/Rich Gabrielson, 5, Icon Sportswire/Rich Graessle, 26, USA
Today Sports/Aaron Doster, 24, ZUMA Press/Carlos Gonzalez, 16, ZUMA Press/Dan
Anderson, 28, ZUMA Press/Jeff Wheeler, 23, ZUMA Press/Jerry Holt, 20; Shutterstock:
winui, 1

All internet sites appearing in back matter were available and accurate when this book
was sent to press.

Direct Quotations
Page 8, "ball skills and concentration..." Dan Gunderson, January 19, 2018, https://www.
mprnews.org/story/2018/01/19/adam-thielen-nfl-vikings-detroit-lakes-minnesota-star,
Accessed on December 18, 2019.

TABLE OF CONTENTS

Glossary terms are **BOLD** on first use.

TOUCHDOWN MAKER!

November 30, 2014, was turning out to be a great day to be a Minnesota Vikings fan. The Vikings led the Carolina Panthers 7–0. Halfway through the first quarter, the Vikings defense forced a Panther punt.

As punter Brad Nortman caught the snap, Vikings backup wide receiver Adam Thielen burst through the offensive line. Thielen leaped into the air and blocked the kick. Lying on the ground, Thielen scooped up the ball and jumped to his feet. He raced 30 yards to the end zone for a touchdown! It was his first NFL score. Thielen was so excited, he jumped into the stands to celebrate with Vikings fans!

Adam Thielen runs the ball into the Vikings end zone after his blocked punt. They beat the Panthers 31–13.

Cris Carter was a Vikings wide receiver from 1990 to 2001.

HOMETOWN HERO

Adam Thielen was like many kids growing up in the tiny town of Detroit Lakes, Minnesota. He loved sports, especially football. As a kid, Thielen would spend hours playing football in the backyard with his friends. He pretended to be Vikings greats Cris Carter and Randy Moss. His mom says that when he was just six years old, Thielen knew he would play in the NFL.

Sports played a big part in Thielen's life. He grew up loving basketball and golf. He even played volleyball with his family. But it was his skills catching a football that would stand out as he got older. He had a gift and a dream—to play for the Minnesota Vikings!

FACT

Thielen isn't just a football star. In 2008, he led his high school golf team to a state championship.

Years of playing backyard football paid off for Thielen when he reached Detroit Lakes High School in 2004. Today, Thielen is 6'2" (188 centimeters) and weighs 200 pounds (91 kilograms). In high school, he was a skinny 160-pound (73-kg) receiver and barely 6-feet (183-cm) tall. Still, he seemed to catch everything thrown his way. A former high school coach said it was Thielen's "ball skills and **concentration**" that made him a superstar.

But in high school, Thielen was more focused
on basketball than football. His plan was to earn a
scholarship to play basketball in college. This didn't
hurt him in the long run. The skills he learned playing
high school basketball made him a better football
player. Going after a rebound is similar to going after
a pass. He mastered battling with a defender for the
ball in two sports.

‹‹‹ Detroit Lakes, Thielen's hometown,
is appropriately named. Over 400 lakes
can be found in and around the town.

CHAPTER TWO

SMALL-TOWN SUPERSTAR

Thielen graduated from high school in June 2008. No colleges offered Thielen a basketball scholarship. He was unsure what would happen next. The four-sport superstar was without a team. No basketball. No football. No scholarships at all. Then he got a call from a small Division II school. It wasn't a football powerhouse like Alabama or Michigan. But it was a home state university. And it was his shot. Thielen went to join the Mavericks of Minnesota State University, Mankato, or MNSU.

Thielen was the best player on his high school team. When he arrived at MNSU, he couldn't even get on the field. Believing he was too small, the coaches sidelined him for the 2008 season. College players take redshirt seasons to develop their skills. His coaches wanted him to get bigger. He needed to get ready for college-level play.

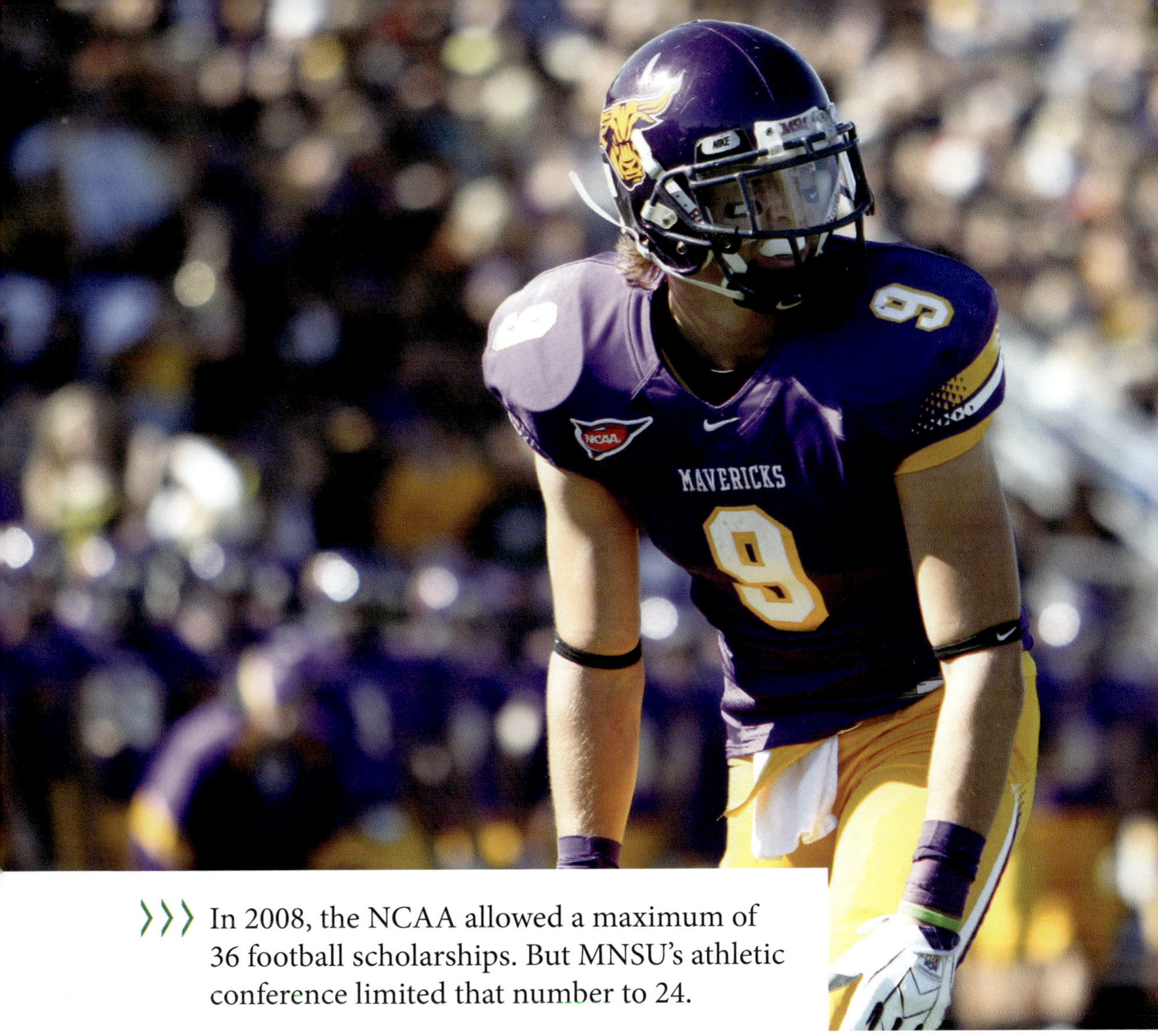

>>> In 2008, the NCAA allowed a maximum of 36 football scholarships. But MNSU's athletic conference limited that number to 24.

FACT

MNSU offered Thielen a $500 scholarship. That wasn't even enough to pay for his schoolbooks.

COLLEGE SUCCESS

Despite his redshirt season, Thielen never lost sight of his goals. The rest of his seasons at MNSU were a success. Thielen had 124 catches for more than 1,600 yards. He focused on taking it one day at a time and believing in himself. That belief paid off. He led the Mavericks in receiving during his sophomore, junior, and senior seasons. His senior year, Thielen caught eight touchdown passes. He hauled in 74 passes for 1,176 yards. At a Division I school, these numbers would have interested NFL **scouts**. But at Division II, he didn't even get an invite to a scouting camp for the NFL.

FACT

Thielen was more than a wide receiver in college. He returned punts and kickoffs. He was even the holder on field goals!

>>> Thielen (9) dodges his opponents from Wayne State College.

A lot of players might have given up. Thielen knew he had to find a way to make his dream come true.

CHAPTER THREE

ROAD TO THE NFL

The national NFL Scouting Combine is held each February in Indianapolis. Scouts from all 32 NFL teams look at players there. They decide who they want to **draft**. Without an invite, Thielen missed the chance to show off his skills.

After the national combine, the NFL holds smaller combines across the country. Players hoping for a miracle go to try out. Thielen paid $275 to attend a combine in Chicago. He knew this might be his only chance, so he trained hard. He studied how to be able to run faster. Scouts look at how fast wide receivers can run a 40-yard dash. A slow time in the dash almost always means a player won't be drafted. Thielen delivered a time of 4.45 seconds. It was enough to earn him an invite to a larger NFL combine. His dream was still alive!

>>> Thielen runs the ball in a 2013 preseason
game against the Tennessee Titans.

After not being invited to the national NFL Combine,
Thielen made a plan for life without football. He was
offered a job with a company to sell dental equipment.

The 2013 NFL Draft was held in New York City. A total of 254 college players were chosen by the 32 NFL teams. Twenty-six wide receivers were drafted. Despite doing well at two regional combines, Thielen wasn't one of them. But two teams showed interest in signing him to a **contract** after the draft. They were the Carolina Panthers and his home state's Minnesota Vikings. On May 6, 2013, the Minnesota Vikings signed the undrafted **rookie** to a three-year contract. Thielen had beat the odds.

Three months later, Thielen hauled in a 10-yard pass
in the Vikings second preseason game of 2013. It was
his first catch in a professional football game. Three
weeks later, the Vikings cut Thielen from the **roster**.

CHAPTER FOUR

NO DRAFT, NO PROBLEM

The NFL is a numbers game. And there wasn't room on the Vikings 53-man roster. Returning wide receivers Greg Jennings and Jerome Simpson had the starting spots locked up. And first-round draft pick Cordarrelle Patterson was expected to do well. Thielen was an unproven kid from a small college. Still, Thielen impressed his coaches in training camp and during the preseason. He worked hard and had a great attitude. A day after he was cut, the team signed him to a secondary roster called the practice squad.

Thielen never played in a single regular season game in 2013. He worked out with the team every day. He watched game film. He studied other teams. He learned from the Vikings coaches. And he patiently waited for his shot to show that he belonged in the NFL.

Thielen hoped to make the Vikings final roster in 2014. Due to NFL rules, he had only one more season on the practice squad. His play during the preseason helped his cause. Thielen collected eight receptions for nearly 100 yards and one touchdown. But it was his hustle on special teams that helped earn him a spot on the roster.

>>> Thielen catches a touchdown pass against the Chicago Bears. The Vikings beat the Bears 13–9.

Thielen played on special teams for all 16 games of the regular season. He helped on 12 tackles covering kicks. Thielen even earned his first NFL award thanks to his special-teams skills. In week 13, he was named the NFC Special Teams Player of the Week!

Special Teams Superstar

Covering kickoffs and punts on special teams is dangerous work. One study found players on special teams were five times more likely to suffer a **concussion**. Still, for many players, special teams is their only shot to play in the NFL. In 2014, Thielen made only eight catches all season. He stayed on the team because he was willing to work hard. He played every game on special teams. That hard work paved the way for his future as a superstar receiver.

CHAPTER FIVE

NFL SUPERSTAR

In 2014 and 2015, Thielen was known for his **dominant** special teams play. But things changed in 2016. Vikings starting quarterback Teddy Bridgewater hurt his knee. He was out before the season began. The team traded for Philadelphia Eagles quarterback Sam Bradford, and he made an instant connection with Thielen. Thielen's game exploded. For the 2016 season, he caught 69 passes for nearly 1,000 yards and scored five touchdowns. It was a turning point in Thielen's career. He had proven to everyone what he had known all along—he belonged in the NFL.

In 2017, Thielen built on his success. The Vikings rewarded him with a new four-year contract! He caught 91 passes for more than 1,200 yards. He was named to his first **Pro Bowl.**

>>> Thielen catches a pass for a 12-yard gain.
The Vikings beat the Los Angeles Rams 24–7.

UNSTOPPABLE

Free agent quarterback Kirk Cousins joined the Vikings in 2018. Fans expected the Vikings offense to be unstoppable. Thielen certainly was. He had a career year. His 113 receptions were fifth best in the league. He finished in the top five in yards and tied for 10th in touchdowns. His success earned him a second Pro Bowl appearance.

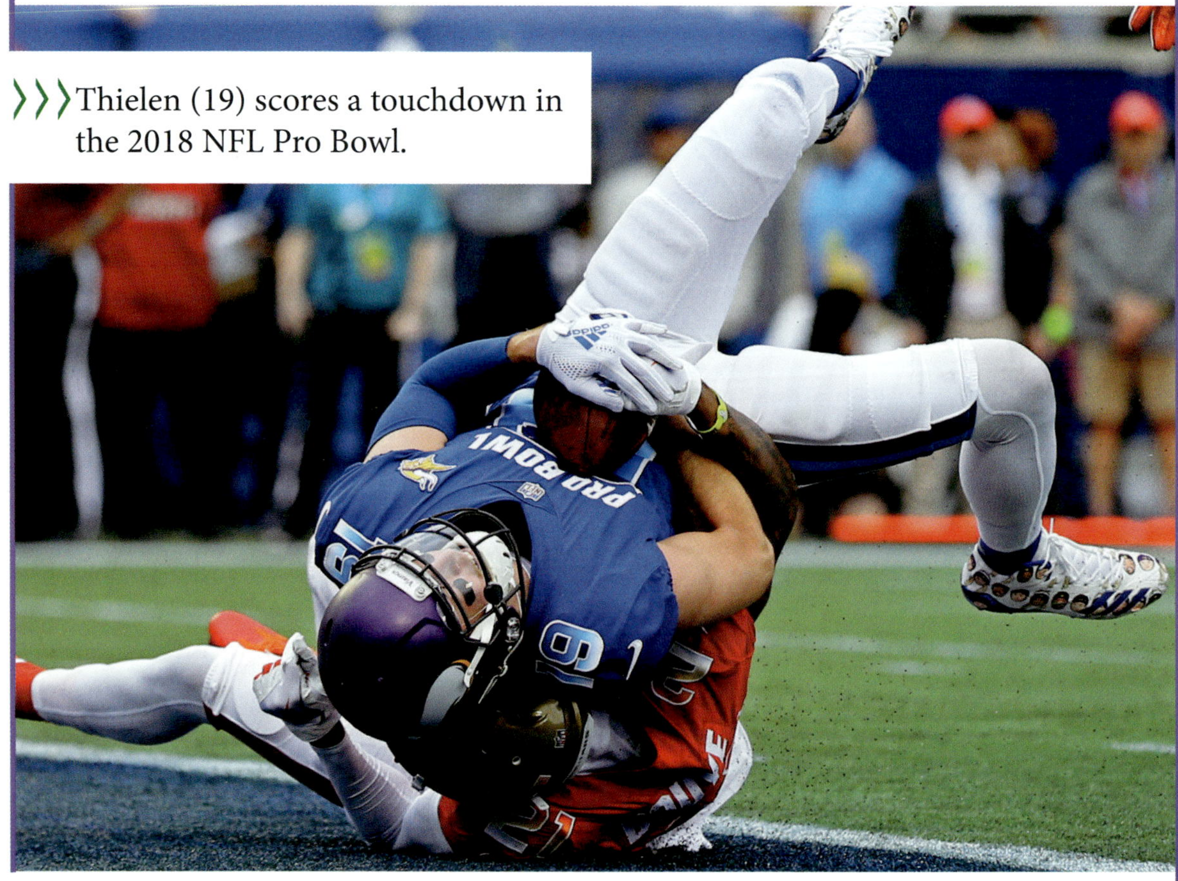

>>> Thielen (19) scores a touchdown in the 2018 NFL Pro Bowl.

After the 2018 season, Thielen was clearly his team's number one receiver. In the offseason, the Vikings added four years to his current contract. The deal was worth $64 million. The player who got a $500 scholarship in college was set to earn millions playing professional football!

Giving Back

In 2018, Thielen took his work off the field to the next level. He and his wife, Caitlin, started the Thielen Foundation. The group focuses on helping children. Thielen shares his passion for football with hundreds of children each year. He holds a free football camp, and he visits hospitals. The foundation also donates toys, food, and other gifts to families in need during the holidays.

Adam Thielen

MIDSEASON INJURY

Hopes were high for the 2019 Vikings. Even though Thielen had his biggest pro season in 2018, the team missed the playoffs.

In the first half of the 2019 season, Thielen struggled. He caught just 27 passes for fewer than 400 yards. Worse still, he injured his **hamstring** midseason. He missed games for the first time since joining the Vikings in 2014. Thielen's 2019 season was a disappointment compared to his 2018 season. Still, the Vikings earned a Wild Card playoff spot.

In the playoffs, he caught seven passes for 129 yards in their first game against the New Orleans Saints. But the magic ended the following week. Thielen, battling injuries, was held to five catches for 50 yards. He came up short, and the Vikings 2019 season was over with the loss.

THE FUTURE IS BRIGHT

In 2019, Thielen was the second-highest paid player on the Vikings roster. He earned more than $16 million that season. But he still has a long road and career ahead. After six years in the league, Thielen has yet to lead his team to the Super Bowl. Still, he is one of the most **dynamic** wide receivers in the game. The future is bright for this hometown star. Fans hope Thielen will soon lead the Vikings to their first Super Bowl win!

TIMELINE

<table>
<tr><td>1990</td><td>Born in Detroit Lakes, Minnesota</td></tr>
<tr><td>2008</td><td>Begins his career as a redshirt freshman with Minnesota State University, Mankato</td></tr>
<tr><td>2013</td><td>Signs a rookie contract with the Minnesota Vikings</td></tr>
<tr><td>2014</td><td>Plays his first season on the active roster; makes his first NFL catch against the Green Bay Packers</td></tr>
<tr><td>2016</td><td>Completes the first 100-yard game of his career; makes seven catches for 127 yards to help beat the Houston Texans 31–13</td></tr>
<tr><td>2017</td><td>Finishes the season, the first 1,000-yard season of his career, with 1,276 receiving yards; earns his first Pro Bowl selection</td></tr>
<tr><td>2017</td><td>Makes his first postseason catch in his second career playoff game; finishes the game with six catches as the Vikings beat the Saints 29–24</td></tr>
<tr><td>2019</td><td>Signs a four-year, $64 million contract extension; gets a guaranteed $35 million</td></tr>
</table>

GLOSSARY

CONCENTRATION (kahn-suhn-TRAY-shuhn)—the ability to direct thought or effort toward a particular task or idea

CONCUSSION (kuhn-KUH-shuhn)—an injury to the brain caused by a hard blow to the head

CONTRACT (KAHN-trakt)—an agreement between people stating the terms by which one will work for the other

DOMINANT (DAH-muh-naynt)—very powerful or important

DRAFT (DRAFT)—the process of choosing a person to join a sports team

DYNAMIC (dye-NAM-ik)—positive in attitude and full of energy and new ways of doing things

HAMSTRING (HAM-string)—a muscle in the thigh that helps to flex and extend the leg

PRO BOWL (PRO BOHL)—a NFL game where the best players from the AFC and NFC play each other

ROOKIE (RUK-ee)—a first-year player

ROSTER (ROSS-tur)—a list of players on a team

SCHOLARSHIP (SKOL-ur-ship)—money given to a student to pay for school

SCOUT (SKOWT)—someone who looks for players who might be able to be professionals

READ MORE

Chandler, Matt. *Football: A Guide for Players and Fans.* North Mankato, MN: Capstone Press, 2020.

Gigliotti, Jim. *Talkin' Football.* Mankato, MN: The Child's World, 2020.

Storm, Marysa. *Highlights of the Minnesota Vikings.* Mankato, MN: Black Rabbit Books, 2020.

INTERNET SITES

Adam Thielen Stats
www.vikings.com/team/players-roster/adam-thielen/

Minnesota Vikings Ring of Honor
www.profootballhof.com/teams/minnesota-vikings/team-greats/

NFL Playoff Picture
www.nfl.com/playoffs/playoff-picture

INDEX